SANCTUARY!

The animal-friendly Coloring Book

by Graham Harrop

ISBN-13: 978-1976576249

If you take
someone's coat
by accident, you
can always
return it. If you
take mine,
it's for keeps!

I got dumped
at the Auto-mall!
If I hadn't learned
how to drive
a stick-shift,
I wouldn't
be here today!

I narrowly escaped
with my life!
When they said
that they were
taking me to
hog heaven,
I believed them!

They told me
that the grass is
greener on the
other side of the
wall and it turns
out that they
were right!

The only lab
I want to see
had big ears
and a
wet nose!

Kids run away
from home to
join a circus!
I ran away from
the circus to
find a home!

People pay to see
me perform.
I'm hoping that
someone will
buy me a ticket
to freedom!

Someone said:
'Animal cruelty
really gets my goat!'
I'm glad that
they came
and got
me!

They say that cats
have nine lives.
I guess my friends
at the lab had
used up their
other eight

1 2 3 4 5 6 7 8 9

So anyway, two
of the crates fall
off the truck
and I find a
new home at
the 'Happy Hen
Bird Sanctuary'!

I'd never seen
grass until I
was rescued!
You can't grow
anything on a
cold cement
floor!

I'm really glad
that we parrots
can talk!
I learned a brand
new word today:
'Freedom!'

I spent time in a
research lab.
I had to play
'Rescue Me!'
27 times before
someone finally
got the hint!

They say that
elephants never
forget.
I only wish
that I could!